The Quest

SUSAN ALLEN PANZICA

Eternity Cafe Publishers

THE QUEST

This book is a work of fiction. Names, characters, businesses, organizations, places, events, and incidents either are the product of the author's imagination or are used fictitiously. Any resemblance to actual persons, living or dead, events, or locales is entirely coincidental.

For information contact :
susan@susanpanzica.com
http://www.susanpanzica.com

Editing by Sally Hanan of Inksnatcher and by Laura Hodges Poole
Book Formatting by Derek Murphy @Creativindie
Book Cover design by AJ Panzica of Zica, Inc.

First Edition: March 2018
ISBN 978-0996803533

To girls—of all ages—deeply loved by the King.

Foreward

Christine and I have been teaching for over 20 years. In that time, we have seen many young people come through our doors. There has always been the occasional student who seemed burdened or hopeless. In recent years, we noticed a pattern of young people engaging in self-destructive behaviors as a means of coping with the struggles that they face. This hopelessness began to present itself in younger and younger students. This project was conceived out of a need to provide a message of hope and healing – the need for a message that counters our culture's deceptive call to self-reliance which leads to isolation.

This story helps us to understand that we are designed to share each other's burdens and uphold each other in times of struggle. Learning to be vulnerable and transparent with one another reminds us that we are not alone. It speaks to us, reminding us that many people face feelings of insecurity, fear, pride, self-reliance, and doubt.

"The message of relying on something greater than ourselves is lost in our culture." Christine Crawley

If we would understand that true healing only comes through a relationship with a God who is greater than we are, we would experience the joy and peace that restores hope.

As dancers and choreographers, Christine and my first form of communication is dance. We are thrilled to have had the privilege of bringing this story to the stage through dance. Susan has brought depth to the characters and provided eloquent and powerful words to the story in *The Quest* – a fairy tale, only with heroes which are very, very real. The truths highlighted in these pages are tools for each of us to embrace so that we can all be victorious in all our struggles. *The Quest* brings to life characters in which we can all see a bit of ourselves. As we watch the characters navigate through this adventure, we are given to opportunity to meet our own personal "knight in shining armor".

So, what do you think? With God on our side like this, how can we lose? If God didn't hesitate to put everything on the line for us, embracing our condition and exposing himself to the worst by sending his own Son, is there anything else he wouldn't gladly and freely do for us? And who would dare tangle with God by messing with one of God's chosen? Who would dare even to point a finger? The One who died for us—who was raised to life for us!—is in the presence of God at this very moment sticking up for us. Do you think anyone is going to be able to drive a wedge between us and Christ's love for us? There is no way! Not trouble, not hard times, not hatred, not hunger, not homelessness, not bullying threats, not backstabbing, not even the worst sins listed in Scripture. None of this fazes us because Jesus loves us. I'm absolutely convinced that nothing—nothing living or dead, angelic or demonic, today or tomorrow, high or low, thinkable or unthinkable—absolutely nothing can get between us and God's love because of the way that Jesus our Master has embraced us. Romans 8:31-39 MSG

What would your life look like if you truly knew how loved you are by The King?

Jessica Morales

Preface

It's not every day that someone comes to you and asks you to write a book for a dance performance. But that's what happened with *The Quest*.

Last year, Jes Morales, her partner Christine Crawford, and the New School of Dance Arts created a performance based on a Max Lucado children's book. This year, they wanted to do a similar program, but larger and deeper in scope. She described the issues girls face in today's society, the need for redemption and a return to the shamelessness of the garden, and how water is a symbol for freedom.

They searched but couldn't find a book that suited their needs. Yet, they weren't about to let that stop them—Jes asked me to write one!

I had countless reasons to say "no." It wasn't my writing genre… I don't work with young girls… I'm extraordinarily busy with other projects. I simply told Jes I'd pray about it. Then I took my dog for a walk.

On the side street where I live, where I've

walked my dog a thousand of times, I came upon a large, newly painted, bright blue metal plate embedded in the pavement. Raised letters embossed the disc: W – A – T – E – R.

Immediately, I felt like God gave the go-ahead to this project—and the ideas started to flow like the water rushing through the pipe underneath the road.

Join us and our heroine, Esperanza, on a journey to discover life transforming truth.

CONTENTS

1

The Village

Was it always this dark in the village? Esperanza wondered, looking at the gray dwellings on each side of the cobblestone lane—windows draped with tattered curtains and not a spot of green in sight, almost as if an acid cloud had drifted through the village and stolen all the color.

The click of her heels on the hard stone path measured each step she took. She hurried out of the gloomy village to visit Prudence—a tiny, wrinkled woman with mahogany brown skin and glacier white hair—who lived in a pristine little cottage at the edge of town near the forest. The bright cottage stood in stark contrast to the dreary thatched-roofed homes that surrounded the village.

Young Esperanza loved the wise old woman dearly, often bringing her warm loaves of bread. Esperanza longed to hear her stories of the days of old, but Prudence rarely spoke of them, and her eyes clouded with mystery whenever Esperanza asked about the legend of the beautiful garden.

As Esperanza quietly opened the heavy wooden door, she spotted Prudence dozing in her big cozy chair. With her head resting on a plush feather pillow, Prudence's eyes skimmed back and forth under closed eyelids.

What was she dreaming about? Esperanza wondered.

Prudence's lips pursed, then she smiled and quietly began to speak. Esperanza strained to listen, perhaps to learn of the days in the garden.

"I will exalt you, my God the King," Prudence

murmured. "I will praise your name forever and ever."[1]

Someday, Esperanza thought, *someday I'll see it with my own eyes.*

Leaving the basket of bread on the thick pine table, Esperanza kissed Prudence on the forehead and quietly slipped out the door.

There at Prudence's gate, sunlight pierced the gloom, bright golden beams streaming through the branches of a large black tree. Esperanza paused, wanting to enjoy the unusual sunny moment before entering the lane to the village. The normally dismal road held a ray of hope as Esperanza entered the puddle of light.

And then just like that, it disappeared.

Percival had stepped into the sunbeam, blocking the light and creating a dark shadow with his towering stature and massive muscles. His crooked smirk bared ivory teeth like a tiger's, and he was ready to pounce.

For years, it seemed that Percival had tracked

Esperanza. She'd see him hovering at the bakery or by the well or near her vegetable patch. The things he said could appear to be kind but always had another, more heartless, meaning. Things like, "Charming tunic you have on today. Makes you look less ordinary."

Esperanza froze, and before Percival could insult her, she hurried back into the cottage.

"What is it, dear?"

Startled, Esperanza spun around to see Prudence sitting up with concern in her eyes.

"It's just . . . um, it's Percival. He's outside, and I don't want to walk with him back into the village. He makes me uneasy." That subtle talent of his made her feel awkward and self-conscious and reminded her of the things she could have said or should have done differently. If only she was smarter or prettier, maybe then she'd have the confidence to look past him.

"My darlin' Esperanza, Percival is a bully, but he's no threat to you. Why, you have greater strength and wisdom than you know." Prudence pointed to the ottoman by her feet. “Have a seat, child. Let’s chat a bit and maybe that ole Percival will move on.”

Esperanza sat by Prudence, her eyes wide with love and admiration. “Oh Prudence, will you tell me about the beautiful garden? And the king who lives there? Is the story true? Sometimes the older villagers whisper about it, but none will speak of it to anyone else.”

Prudence hesitated, as she always did when Esperanza pressed her for stories of the garden. She sighed deeply and closed her eyes for a moment. When she opened her eyes, she looked straight at her young friend with a scrutiny Esperanza didn’t understand. With a slow nod, Prudence broke off two pieces of the warm bread Esperanza had brought and took a deep breath. “This smells delicious, dear.” She handed one piece to Esperanza. “Maybe you’re ready now. Do you have time for a story?”

“Of course, I do!” Esperanza nearly exploded with joy, sending the bread skyward and crumbs everywhere.

"Please bring me that book over there—the large one on the bookshelf with the gold-edged pages."

Esperanza lifted the heavy book and carried it over to Prudence. Her heart was racing, so she took special care to move with reverence. To her surprise, Prudence didn't open the book. She sat it on her lap and placed her hand gently on the leather cover. She closed her eyes, appearing to get lost in her reverie.

And then she began.

"Once upon a time, in a land not so far away, a wonderful king lived with his royal subjects. The people loved their king, for he governed with wisdom, judged with mercy, loved with grace, and ruled with compassion. Their land was a magical garden filled with beauty, peace, and harmony.

"The flowers bloomed bright crimson, violet, and goldenrod. Abundant plants bursting with fruits and vegetables sustained all the people. Every kind of beast and animal strolled to and fro together in perfect harmony across the garden.

"From the top of the mountain flowed a wide

river of azure blue—crystal clear and twinkling like diamonds as the sun sparkled on its surface. Along its way, a gushing waterfall crested over a ridge and splashed into a deep cerulean pool before peacefully winding on through the garden.

"Beside the river, right in the middle of the garden, stood a colossal tree—providing both shade and sustenance. Everything was perfect.

"Or so it seemed."

Prudence paused; a flicker of grief crossed her face.

"A snake slithered along the garden path and came to rest in the giant tree. Jealous of how the people loved the king, the snake was greedy, wanting his own way and wishing others to follow him. Oh, that snake was shrewd and cunning. Yes, clever with knowledge but without wisdom.

"His lies tricked the people so that they disobeyed their kind king. They began to have notions of their own wisdom, shallow though it was. They thought they only needed themselves and lost all sense of community. Their hearts grew hard and fearful, and they were no longer able to see the beauty around them. Because of their disobedience, they were banished from the garden to live in a dark, bleak village outside the garden walls.

"In the village filled with shadows, the people grew lonely and suspicious. They stopped trusting each other and sometimes hurt each other. Their hearts felt a mysterious loss, but they didn't know what it was that they were missing.

"As the years passed, the people almost forgot about the garden and their wise and wonderful king. Like a dream, their long-lost memory faded into a legend. They sometimes wondered if it was ever real.

"But, child, it was real. As real as this bread we are eating." Prudence took a sip of water. Then, with a gentle jolt as a new, sudden thought surprised her, Prudence pointed her finger at Esperanza and added, "Wherever you are, my dear, remember you will be given everything you need. Listen for the water, and let it guide you."

"The water? Prudence, whatever do you mean? Please, oh please, tell me more."

Prudence closed her eyes and rested her head back. A wistful smile spread across her face. "My dear, that's all for today. I will see you tomorrow, and we can speak some more."

2

The Adversary

Percival's eyes glared and his fists clenched as he spun on one heel to head back to the village center. He kicked some rocks into the air, then kicked a baby rabbit headlong into the brambles alongside the road, *grrr*ing under his breath.

He couldn't believe the girl had slipped through his fingers again. How he hated to be robbed of an opportunity to impart his worldly influence over her. If she could see all he had to offer, she'd be less skittish when he was around. It was so easy for him to keep others under his spell. All he had to do was tell them what they thought they wanted to hear.

Whatever would he do about her? First of all, he needed to keep the girl away from that wrinkled old bat, Prudence, and that book of hers. She'd be sure to keep feeding Esperanza with her stories. *Oh, but my stories are so much more interesting,* he thought with a snicker.

He found people like Prudence very annoying. They seemed humble, yet so confident they know the truth. Stupid people they were, refusing to recognize the superior influence he could have on their lives.

If they'd let him, he'd see to it that they would succeed even if they had to tell a few white lies. And that's all that should matter to them. Worry about the here and now, not the hereafter, he always said.

Why, they wouldn't have to worry about anything if he was in control! Unless, of course, he wanted them to—which he often did, because worrying would keep their focus on themselves. And that's right where he wanted them.

Percival was determined that the villagers would remain under his influence, especially girls like Esperanza, who should always feel inferior, blinded to their true beauty and talents.

Wasn't Esperanza like other girls her age? He knew how to treat them. Keep them feeling secretly lonely, even if in a crowd, like no one understood them. Or keep them isolated and make them think that was the best way to be—independent, liberated, self-sufficient! He was very proficient in this deception—most never knew they were created to live in community with each other, or to help and encourage each other.

The villagers kept their eyes downcast as they went about their errands. Avoiding eye contact reinforced the falsehood that they were alone.

But outliers like Prudence and Esperanza puzzled and irritated Percival. His tactics and schemes, so effective with others, only distanced himself from them. Oh, if only people didn't have a free will of their own! It was beyond his power to force that will to do his bidding.

He approached a curve in the road leading to the village, *his* village, and smelled the village before he saw it. The delightful smell of decay. He breathed in deeply, pushed his shoulders back, and puffed his chest out. He lifted his chin and stepped through the village gate with one arm on his hip and buttons practically popping off the front of his shirt. His brawn would please the foolish damsels who saw no further than people's outer appearances.

Enjoying the admiration of the villagers, he strode through the town square, past the village well, and into the local tavern, where the barkeep immediately sent over his favorite brew.

"Here you go, Percival! Warm, dark ale, just how you like it!"

Seated at his special reserved table, Percival glanced at the barkeep and took a swig. Then he turned to gaze out the window. His eyes didn't miss much as they surveyed the harried villagers going about their tasks.

The bakery stood directly across from the tavern, its large front window topped by a faded pink and formerly white-striped, tattered awning. Inside, Mrs. Baker and her lanky husband looked flustered as they gathered their many children, who squawked around them like chickens in a coop. The littlest one ran in circles, slipping through her mother's arms like she was slathered in butter. Wisps of Mrs. Baker's hair escaped from under her cap, and she kept wiping her forehead with her forearm to keep the strands out of her eyes.

Percival took quiet satisfaction in Mrs. Baker's distress. His subtle jabs at her weight kept her overly sensitive about it. Whenever the newspaper published a story about an attractive woman who accomplished something noteworthy, he was sure to stop by the bakery and "kindly" drop off a copy with a smile. His goal to keep her insecure was right on track.

The village mayor strolled out of the bakery, a haphazard bundle of papers under his arm. His short legs could barely support his rotund belly, and he looked like he might pitch forward into the mud.

"Hmmph, hmmph, hmmph!" Shaking his head at no one in particular, he nearly ran into the seamstress at the door to her shop. "Watch where you're going! Don't you know who I am! *Hmmph!*"

"Excuse me, Mr. Mayor! I'm sorry. I didn't see you coming."

"Well, don't let it happen again, or you'll really be sorry!"

Percival smiled. *That pompous fool—so impressed with himself, yet he has nothing impressive about him—his talk is all a big cover to try to conceal his sense of inadequacy.*

A few shops down from the bakery and seamstress, Percival watched Mr. Smith working wearily over the white-hot forge as the horses waited for their new shoes. His apprentice, Micah, brushed the horses before clearing out the soiled hay beneath them.

Percival sputtered. "Can't stand that kid."

Micah was a fine-looking teenager with olive skin, darktousled curls, and a heart of integrity—a wonderful catch for any young lady, if she would give him a chance.

Micah looked up as two girls strolled out of the cobbler's shop, passing the blacksmith's open doors. They hurried by with their hands over their noses. Percival laughed. He kept the village girls focused on Micah's dusty clothes and distasteful smell. And Micah spent lonely days and nights with horses as his best friends.

Percival's eyes roamed the town square. All the merchants and peasants, schoolgirls and boys, tradesmen, farmers, and villagers of all social strata wore a similar dreary look. Thanks to Percival, they went through the motions of life but without the spark of life.

Ha! What these fluff-headed folks forgot was their capacity to strengthen and uplift each other, to bear each other's burdens. Who knew how joyful they could be if only they'd take their eyes off themselves? Instead Percival made them suspicious of one another, thinking they could and should brave life on their own, drawing upon some inner strength that eluded them.

He wore a self-satisfied half smile, but not for long.

His thoughts drifted back to Esperanza. What a great catch she would be for him. How he'd love to destroy that pathetic core of hope that sustained her through her darkest days. He slammed his beer stein down, splashing foam on the thick oak table and cobblestone floor. Then, to no one in particular, he said, "Lucky for me, she doesn't know there are others like her."

"Everything okay, Percival?"

Percival turned away from the window to see a tall, somber fellow by his table. Ah! Henrick, his faithful sidekick. "What do you want?"

"Just checkin' on ya, man. You seem a little frustrated."

"Frustrated? Ha! You're crazy! I've got

everything under control."

"Do you?"

"What are you talking about?"

"I know you're grumbling about those outliers." He lifted his chin toward the window. "Drives you crazy that you can't, shall we say, *persuade* them all."

Percival took a long gulp of his ale, gently placing the thick glass stein back on the table in a herculean effort to maintain his composure. He plastered a smirk on his face and looked up at Henrick.

"Henrick, seriously, you are quite mistaken. Those few outliers will see the light, my light, soon enough."

"Your darkness, you mean? Ha-ha!"

"Whatever you want to call it."

Henrick was almost right. Percival was more than frustrated! Rage simmered in his gut. Those outliers reminded him of his only real opponent—the one who refused to share the limelight, the one who saw him for who he truly was, the one who ejected him from the garden. His nostrils flared, and his jaw clenched at the memory.

But he'd gotten even, all right! All these lost souls in the village, all so precious to the king, all now barely remembered him. Percival spat on the floor. Ha! It wouldn't be long before they totally forgot the king, and who he originally made them to be. Percival took a deep breath.

Well, not *all* the lost souls. His jaw clenched again.

But it won't be long. Soon, I'll have my way. Soon, I'll snare each one. Soon, they'll see the light.

Or the darkness, if you prefer.

3

The Dream

T***hat night, as Esperanza laid her head on her pillow,*** visions of the garden twirled in her head.

Paths cut gently through flowery meadows. The beauty surrounding her made her feel lighter than air. Esperanza breathed deeply, delighting in the scent of crimson roses on her right mingling with lemons from the grove on her left. Before her lay miles of lush greenness.

In the distance, sunlight radiated from a

plateau at the top of a mountain. A waterfall rushed over the mountain's edge, cascading into a pool, which lead to a crystal stream that flowed through the garden.

Esperanza felt a freedom she had never known, yet she was drawn toward the mountain as if an invisible tether pulled her. Her destiny was there, at the top of that mountain.

Suddenly, Esperanza was not alone. She saw herself as one of a trio of lithe, lovely ladies dancing down flowered paths. The wind whipped their skirts as the girls meandered their way in colorful bliss. The sound of rushing water called them farther into the garden, each step bringing them closer to a sense of belonging.

The swoosh of powerful wings overhead made them look up. An enormous eagle sailed above effortlessly, gliding over the meadows and coming to rest on the back of a powerful lion ascending the mountain toward the glowing light. The lion wore a magnificent jeweled golden crown.

As the trio continued on its journey, the colors began to dim. The sky clouded over, and the vision of the garden melted away like wax too close to a fire. The gurgling of the water drew them on . . . but now the sound came from the dreary village they were approaching. The garden trail became a harsh stone path leading to the village well.

And then Esperanza heard it—a voice so kind, it gently sliced through the darkness.

"My dear Esperanza, listen for the water. I have given you everything you need—at the well."

She startled awake and sat bolt upright. The well! "Everything I need is at the well!" Prudence said she'd be given everything she needed, and now she knew where to find it.

She had no idea what it was she needed, but she felt certain she was about to find out. She got dressed and ran so fast toward the village center that she stumbled and nearly fell flat on her face.

When the well finally came into view, she stopped short and squinted to see more clearly. *Who are* they*? And* what *are they doing there*? Two young maidens in the place where she alone was supposed to be. Or so she thought.

The short lass sat on the cobblestone bench beside the well, the toes of her boots scribbling in the dust below. The tall one slowly circled the well, looking up, down, and all around for something that eluded her.

Esperanza picked up her speed again and approached the well with furrowed brow and puzzled eyes.

"Did you hear it too?" the tall girl asked as she stopped circling the well and, with hands on hips, stared straight at Esperanza.

"Hear what?" Esperanza replied.

The tall girl pointed to the lass on the bench. "We both had a dream last night—a dream about a king who lives in a magical garden."

Esperanza's mouth dropped open.

"The garden was beautiful—filled with flowers of every color and a river flowing through it from a waterfall. And a voice in the garden told us to come to the well, where we would have everything we needed."

Barely finding her voice, Esperanza squeaked out, "Wha-a-at? Who are you?"

"I'm Mai-Lyn. And this is Sienna. Who are you?"

"I'm Esperanza. I also had a dream last night about the garden. And I heard the voice tell me that everything I needed was at the well. But here I am, and I don't see anything different than any other day. Except that you are here."

They might have had the same dream, but that's where their similarities stopped.

Mai-Lyn stood tall, agile, and muscular with a mass of glossy jet-black hair trailing down her back, begging to be tamed. Every move she made exhibited graceful strength and power. If she'd held a spear, she could have been mistaken for a samurai warrior.

Sienna was not just short; she was diminutive in every way. Her spectacles slipped halfway down her slender nose, and her straw-blonde hair, loosely knotted in a bun, but uncontrolled, judging by the countless flyaway strands that created a glistening halo around her head.

Esperanza flipped her curly chestnut hair over her shoulder, wishing she was taller or shorter or anything but average. People remarked that her splendid inner beauty radiated across her face, but of course, she couldn't see any of that.

The other two girls stared at her. How could they all have had the same dream about the garden? And what could it possibly mean that everything they needed was at the well?

Well, there was only one way to find out.

Esperanza looked around the cobblestone square. The well sat in the middle, surrounded by wooden buckets and stone benches. To her right, the baker, the seamstress, the cobbler, and the blacksmith were all setting up their stores for the day. To her left, through the tavern windows, she saw the barkeeper wiping tables after a long night of people drowning their sorrows in ale.

"Well, the garden surely isn't here." She looked at her companions. "It looks like we need to leave the village, don't we? If we're to listen for the water to lead us, that path over there leads to the stream."

The girls took their first steps down the hard stone path out of the village on their journey to find the magical garden and the king who dwelt there.

Esperanza felt her knees get wobbly and her stomach flip. Prudence's cottage was as far as she had ever traveled. Now she was not just leaving the village to embark on a journey to a mysterious garden that may or may not exist, but she was traveling with two strangers. The enormity of this expedition suddenly swept over her. She stopped walking.

Mai-Lyn spun toward her. "You're not backing out, are you?" she demanded.

"No," Esperanza tugged at the hem of her

blouse. “Ehh, no, I'm not backing out. But I need a moment to think, to process what we’re doing. I’ve lived in the village all my life, but I’ve never seen you two before. At least, I don’t think I have. Maybe we should talk before we walk?”

Mai-Lyn’s onyx black eyes bored into Esperanza’s. She put one hand on her hip and started to raise a pointed finger at Esperanza before dropping it to her side. Mai-Lyn appeared used to getting her own way, but she began speaking a bit more softly, her two hands extended palms up toward each of the other girls.

“Separately, we each had the same dream, right? —a dream with a message, a dream that instructed us what to do. Don’t you think that even if it’s bizarre, this is a real situation we’re in? And so, shouldn’t we follow the instructions?” She raised both her arms and spun around, “I can’t wait to get out of this village! The people are like zombies. They’re literally the walking dead!”

Esperanza looked at Sienna. She had sat down

on a rock beside the path and was reaching out to some chipmunks scurrying in and out of the rocks. Miraculously, the chipmunks stopped their race and paused to look at her tiny palm that offered some acorns. With her arm extended, her sleeve shifted and Esperanza saw faint scars, short thin lines across the soft underside of her forearm.

The chipmunks grabbed the acorns and ran off as if they had just stolen the crown jewels. Sienna yanked down her sleeve. Esperanza realized that up until now, Mai-Lyn had done all the talking for the duo, so she spoke directly to Sienna. “What do you think about all this?”

Sienna turned toward her new companions and closed her eyes. Then slowly opened them, and with a voice as delicate as her stature, she spoke. “I have always felt something was out there beyond our village. But I would never have considered straying from my district, my home. My books have been my closest friends, and I couldn’t leave them.

“Then I had the dream. In it, I saw a vision of

real, authentic beauty. And when I heard the voice telling me to go to the well, I felt a stirring inside me, as if a supernatural power gripped me.

"When I got near the well, I saw Mai-Lyn and I turned back. She reminded me of someone I'd known before . . . a girl who often . . . bullied me." Her words dropped off, and her voice got softer, if that had been possible. It looked like she might cry, but she shook her head and continued.

"But I remembered the power I felt from the voice in the dream, and so I turned back and made it to the well. When Mai-Lyn said that she had the same dream, I knew there really was something extraordinary going on that I was called to be a part of."

Esperanza envied these two. One embodied stunning natural strength and beauty. The other seemed filled with both knowledge and wisdom. Esperanza felt herself to be plain and common. If her companions thought so, they kept it to themselves, but their assurance pierced her insecurity. She felt stronger being in their company. The quest to find the truth about the garden had been her lifelong dream. Perhaps the dream wasn't hers alone.

4

The Woods

T***he lane out of the village*** took them past Prudence's small cottage. Leaning on her crooked cane, Prudence stood by the path just inside her gate. Esperanza ran ahead to hug her dear friend, words gushing out faster than one would think possible.

"We're going to find the garden, Prudence! Oh my! After you told me the story, I had the most beautiful dream. A voice told me to go to the well. And so I did, and there they were!" Esperanza stretched out her arm to her companions. "Mai-Lyn, Sienna, and I met at the well. And we each had the same dream! We each dreamed about the garden, and the king, and a voice telling us to go to the well. Can you imagine that?"

"Yes, my precious one." A faint smile curled Prudence's lips as she gently nodded and looked at the trio and then up to the sky. "Yes, I sure can imagine that."

"It's all so strange! I've wanted this for so long, but never dreamed it could really happen. I'm so excited, but a bit frightened too."

"Remember, Esperanza. You will be given everything you need. Listen for the water, and remember: *'The king always keeps his promises; he is gracious in all he does. He grants the desires of those who fear him; he hears their cries for help and rescues them.'*[2] These words will help you in time of need.

"And please, my dear, take this belt." Prudence extended her arm and offered the sturdy leather belt in her frail, wrinkled hand. "It has meant so much to me over the years, and I want you to have it with you on your journey."

Esperanza stared at the treasured intricate belt—carefully tooled leather with a shining golden buckle. It felt heavy and cumbersome until she buckled it around her waist, when it felt lighter than air.

The two friends hugged farewell; then she, Mai-Lyn, and Sienna waved goodbye. As Prudence slowly turned toward her cottage, Esperanza thought she saw a tear glisten alongside a deep wrinkle in Prudence's leathery brown cheek.

The path led them to a streambed, but the dust and deep cracks indicated it had dried up long ago. With no water there, they continued on until they reached a dark, wooded thicket. Surely there'd be water there to nourish all the greenery!

Trees of all sizes and shapes greeted them. As the trio traveled deeper into the forest, the foliage appeared to shift in mystical motion. The grass shrank in the shadows of the growing leaves. The trees stood erect with tall, elongated trunks. They appeared to form a maze, from which there was no escape. The girls lost sight of their direction and destination as they focused on the trees, which seemed to torment them.

The wind howling through the trees teased them, whispering words of defeat and despair. The leaves flapped hysterically as if to mock their very presence. The wind seemed to accuse them.

"Who-o-o-o are *you*?"

"Shhhh-a-m-e..."

The girls clung to each other. The wind's whispers reminded Esperanza of her fears, flaws, and failings. She began to doubt the wisdom of starting on their journey. *Was there really even a garden to discover?*

"We're lost! Why did you go this way?" Sienna's voice trembled.

"Don't blame me. It's not *my* fault!" Mai-Lyn flared at the others.

Esperanza had heard enough. "Well, who's fault

is it?"

From its perch high atop the tallest tree, the sweet chirp of a nightingale pierced the gloom. It seemed to be calling them, urging them to look up. The trio tilted their heads back, taking their eyes off their timber tormenters and focusing on their new friend. Bits of sapphire-blue sky and cottony white puffs of clouds appeared between the tree branches.

Mai-Lyn scaled a nearby tree like a squirrel. She slowed as she neared the top so as not to disturb their bird buddy. Once she reached the peak, she put her hand up to her brow and gazed out over the treetops.

Something glittered in the sunlight. Scrambling to get a better look, Mai-Lyn found a shiny helmet nestled in the branches. She looked down at her new friends, closed her eyes, and lifted her head. Then she took a deep breath and placed the helmet on her head. She turned left and right, and there in the distance, she saw a fusion of colors.

Squinting for a better look, Mai-Lyn let out a shriek of happiness, and the bird fluttered away. Her arm pointing east, she shouted down, "There it is! Oh girls, I can see it! The garden, the river, the waterfall. It's just as we dreamed!"

Mai-Lyn climbed back down the tree, eager to share her discovery. "I wish you could see what I saw! If only you could see beyond this dark, threatening maze!" She shared the helmet with Sienna and then with Esperanza.

The moment they put on the piece of armor, their fears subsided. From their vantage point, they couldn't glimpse the garden with their eyes, yet they possessed newfound hope that they were on the right course. The trio turned and set out eastward.

After their first few steps, they stopped abruptly. Esperanza rubbed her eyes for a better look. The trees, which previously had appeared to be a confusing maze, had actually been lined up in rows like soldiers at attention. A slight shift in the girls' position created a whole new perspective, and they were now able to see their surroundings clearly.

To their surprise, they spotted an old beggar

ambling through a row of trees. Wearing a long, brown, hooded cloak, he carried a stick that could have been a cane or a shepherd's staff. He turned toward them with a nod and a smile that lit up his face, then continued on his way.

While staring toward the exiting vagabond, a new sound caught their attention. A gurgling trickle of water splashed their ankles. *Listen for the water.* Esperanza remembered Prudence's advice and the voice in her dream. She urged her companions to carry on.

"Let's follow this brook. It will surely lead us out of this maze and toward the garden!"

The brook did, indeed, lead them out of the darkness and along a lush path. They practically skipped in delight. Could anything stop them now?

Apparently, yes.

5

The Labyrinth

The path came to an abrupt halt. A vertical wall of massive boulders lay before them. The brook to their right and a steep stone mountain to their left made it impossible to continue. Tufts of green weeds and gray moss spotted the striated rock wall—evidence the stones had been there for many years.

Sienna craned her neck to see the top of the wall. "What will we do now? The wall is too high. It's part of the mountain. We can't possibly continue!"

"Oh yes, we can!" Nothing was going to stop

Mai-Lyn from continuing her journey. Using both her hands and feet, she deftly began to scramble up the rocks.

Esperanza and Sienna watched Mai-Lyn scale the wall without looking back. They looked at each other.

"Do you think Mai-Lyn will return for us?" Sienna murmured.

"I don't know. Should we try to climb the wall?" Carefully, Esperanza stepped onto a protruding rock and tried to grip other rocks with her hands. She climbed about two feet off the ground before losing her footing, lurching backwards off the wall, and landing on her rump. "It's too slippery for me. I don't have what it takes."

Sienna ambled over to the brook. She waded in looking to her left. "I don't see a way around this wall." She returned to Esperanza. "If we can't go around it, and we can't climb over it, we will have go through it."

Esperanza shook her head. "Go through it?

That's not possible!"

"What is our choice? Return to the village?"

Esperanza felt a sharp sting, and then another, and then a whole barrage as pebbles rained down on them. The girls looked up to see Mai-Lyn carefully descending the wall. When she stood before them, Sienna said, "We thought you were gone for good."

Esperanza added, "I didn't imagine you would back for us."

"I wasn't . . . at first." Mai-Lyn looked down at her feet.

"What changed? Why did you turn back?" Esperanza looked confused.

Mai-Lyn kept looking at her foot, now scuffing one back and forth. "Well, it was harder than I thought to go it alone. When I slowed down, I got to thinking. Remember the dream? *Our* dream? The one with *three* girls on the journey? Well, I looked around." She looked up at Esperanza and Sienna. "There I was, alone. Not three. Just one. I didn't want to admit it, but I knew I was supposed to be with you."

Esperanza reached out and placed a hand on her arm. "You're so strong, Mai-Lyn. Thank you for coming back for us."

"You're welcome." Mai-Lyn looked down again, then back up. The buckle of Esperanza's belt glinted in the sunlight and caught Mai-Lyn's eye. "But strong? That's what I want everyone to think," she swallowed hard, "but it's not really true. I try to make others feel small to make myself look better. At least in my own eyes."

Mai-Lyn lifted her skirt to reveal a large gash on her leg. Blood dripped from the wound, and bruises had started to form around it. "I'm not so strong. Ha! This hurts more than I want to admit."

"Oh dear!" Sienna examined Mai-Lyn's leg and ran over to the rock wall. She scoured the rocks, touching all the tufts of moss and weeds, apparently looking for something in particular. "Here it is! I thought I saw this before." Sienna gently lifted a prickly bit of greenery by its roots. She brought it over to the girls, grabbed one of the fleshy spikes, and broke it off. She squeezed the spear over Mai-Lyn's wound. Clear gel oozed out.

When the gel touched her wound, Mai-Lyn recoiled. "It's so cold!" But in a moment, she started laughing. "What *is* that? My leg feels so much better already!"

Sienna adjusted her glasses. "It's aloe vera, a succulent plant with healing properties. You can only find it in dry rocky places like this."

Esperanza ripped off the end of her sleeve and wrapped the cloth around Mai-Lyn's leg.

Mai-Lyn looked at her two companions. "I don't know what to say."

Esperanza glanced sideways at her, "You could try thank you,"

"Thank you."

Sienna went back over to the wall. She peered intently above where she had found the plant. "See that boulder there?" She pointed to a large stone that seemed to face a different direction than the ones around it. "There, beside that stone, is a crevice I think I can fit through. It's hard to see because it's in the shadows, but maybe we each can fit through it."

Esperanza and Mai-Lyn came over and stood before the wall where Sienna had pointed. They joined their hands together to make a step. Sienna stepped onto their hands with one foot and then slid into the crevice with the other.

"What do you see, Sienna?" Mai-Lyn peered inside.

"Um, well, it's dark in here. Shadows are everywhere. It's steep on each side. It's a dreadfully tight space, but . . . but this crevice seems to keep going."

Mai-Lyn clapped her hands. "If there are shadows, it's because there is light. I saw gaps in the rocks when I climbed up the wall."

"Yes!" exclaimed Sienna. "There are a few streams of light farther down. Oh my! Maybe we *can* do this! Yes! We can make it *through* the wall!" Sienna turned around and stretched her hand to the girls. "Come! Follow me—this way!"

Esperanza reached up and grasped Sienna's extended hand while Sienna gripped a boulder with her other hand. Mai-Lyn pushed Esperanza from behind, and with a grunt and a shove, Esperanza slid sideways into the narrow crevice.

Mai-Lyn deftly scaled the wall and quickly joined her two companions. The conduit was so narrow, Mai-Lyn put the helmet on her head, as she wouldn't have fit through with it beside her and she needed both hands free to scramble along the crevice.

Esperanza placed her right foot on a small protrusion and gripped two tiny ledges above her head. She brought her left foot up to the ledge and then carefully moved one hand, then the other, before sliding her right foot to the next protruding rock. The rock felt firm under the ball of her foot. Her face and torso were so close to the rock wall, its strength emanated through her. As she continued, she used both her arms and legs to hoist herself up one ledge, then down the next, pausing to rest and reset her position. She learned to push with her legs rather than pull with her arms, allowing her to move with greater power. Despite her fatigue, scrapes, and bruises, Esperanza felt fortified and empowered rather than depleted and weakened.

Ahead of her, Sienna glided across the wall. For someone so apparently fragile, she demonstrated remarkable dexterity and strength. They didn't talk much for fear of using too much energy, but every once in a while, Mai-Lyn shouted a bit of encouragement to keep their momentum: "You've got this!" "You're doing fine." "That's the way!" She seemed to know just when to share to refill their depleted spirits.

The girls maneuvered over boulders, wedged their bodies around rock formations, and shimmied in and out of gaps, all the while trying to keep focused on the light ahead. Finally, the crevice widened—slowly at first, but then broad beams of light replaced the narrow slivers, and the girls could stand side by side. They hobbled along as the opening came into view. Squinting in the bright sun, they picked up their pace as their excitement spurred them to the finish line. They exploded out the crevice exit onto a grassy knoll, where they each fell down—exhausted, but laughing hysterically.

As their laughter ebbed, they rolled over from their backs to their stomachs and faced each other. Mai-Lyn crossed her arms on top of the helmet, using it as a pillow. "I didn't think we'd make it through! Really, I didn't!"

"You were incredible!" Esperanza's eyes glistened.

"We *all* were incredible!" A tear slipped down Sienna's cheek.

Mai-Lyn sat up. "What is it, Sienna? What's wrong?"

"Nothing is wrong. For the first time in my life, things are starting to go right." She rolled onto her back and stared up at the cloudless sky. "It feels good to feel alive. I've been numb for a long time." She rubbed her forearm. "For an awfully long time."

Esperanza sat up and scooted over to Sienna. Wordlessly, she placed her hand on Sienna's arm. Sienna turned to her, then looked at Mai-Lyn.

"Mai-Lyn, you look like a girl I know. A girl with a lot of friends. Who all hated me. I don't know why they hated me, but either they ignored me when I walked by, or they snickered about me loud enough for me to hear. They made me feel even smaller than I already do.

"One day in my kitchen, I cut myself accidentally. I pressed hard on the cut, and when I focused on the pain of the cut, it dulled the pain I felt inside. I began to cut myself on purpose to dull my emotions."

Mai-Lyn wiped a tear that seeped from her eye.

"I lost myself in my books." Sienna looked up at the sky. "The worlds I read about became the world I lived in. It took a while, but recently, I realized that I wasn't hurting anybody but myself. Now when I feel the need to cut myself, I start writing; I write in my journal, or I write poetry. But I still feel terribly lonely." Her tears started to flow.

Now Mai-Lyn moved over to Sienna and Esperanza. "I'm sorry to say, but I know that girl—the girl who hurt you. Well, I don't actually know *her*, but I know I can be like her." Mai-Lyn looked at her hands, wringing them. "I have been like her."

Sienna wiped her tears and focused her attention on Mai-Lyn.

Mai-Lyn looked up and met her gaze. "I thought making others feel small would make me feel better about myself. And on the surface, it did. But deep down, it only made me feel worse. I learned how to bully others because I was bullied myself—by the people who were supposed to love me." Her voice faltered. "Whenever I left my house, I put on a false bravado as a façade to hide what happened at home. I'd do anything I could to get attention. It's all so embarrassing now. I can't believe I'm telling you this. You won't tell anyone, will you?"

Esperanza shook her head. "Who would we tell? We're all wounded in our own ways."

"You?" exclaimed Sienna. "You seem to have it all together. You're smart and kind. And beautiful."

Esperanza snorted. "Beautiful? Smart? Oh my, you really are exhausted!"

Sienna shook her head. "No, really! That's how I see you."

"That's not how I see me! You two are the beautiful and smart ones. I'm so plain and ordinary. I feel like I'm invisible. Like I'm lost in a game of hide-and-seek, only no one is looking for me."

"Well, my friend, you are *not* invisible. I see you clearly, and seeing you has made me stronger." Sienna put her hand on top of Esperanza's.

Mai-Lyn reached over and put her hand on top of the other two. "I'm glad I came back. I don't think I've ever been this honest with anyone before. In fact, I'm not sure I've ever been honest at all before."

The three girls lay on their backs, heads together, watching the clouds roll in.

Pricks like tiny needles started stinging their arms. Each prick brought new doubts about reaching their destination. Then the pricks turned into pelts and the pelts into a pummel of hail. As the storm grew, apprehension filled the air.

6

The Storm

T**he drops of hail reminded Esperanza** of the lies, accusations, and deceptions she'd heard in the maze of trees and in their village for years before. The three girls hugged their arms and bowed their heads, but the patter continued unabated.

Sienna jumped up. "Shelter!" Her tender voice could barely be heard over the tumult of the hailstones, but she pointed toward a cave cleft out of an enormous boulder, and the girls dashed for protection.

Once inside the damp, dark cave, they sat down in exhaustion. Drips from stalactites echoed through the cavern, creating little puddles across the muddy floor. As the storm raged on, the trio faced a new set of doubts and fears. Esperanza recalled the taunts she had heard from Percival. *Was there any truth to them?* She felt so plain and ordinary. What had made her think she could attempt a journey like this?

The storm's intensity grew so that hailstones, now flying sideways, entered the cave.

"We can't stay here," Mai-Lyn said.

The others agreed, but to go out into the storm would have been impossible, so the girls turned to venture deeper into the cave.

"That's not the way to go."

Esperanza instantly recognized that deep, baritone voice, and her body tensed. *What is Percival doing* here, *of all places*? The trio looked back toward the cave entrance. There he stood, once again blocking any light that managed to enter the cave.

"Oh hello, Percival." Esperanza forced a weak smile and spoke in the most cheerful voice she could muster. "We were just exploring this cavern."

"Well, thanks for sharing, half-pint." Percival's eyes roamed from one girl to the next. "You must have mistaken me for someone who cares."

Mai-Lyn stepped forward, shoulders set, hands on hips. Her eyes squinted and focused squarely on Percival with a little distrust and a lot of admiration. "Who are you, and why are you here?" she said in her sternest voice.

Before he could answer, Esperanza grabbed Mai-Lyn's hand and quietly warned her, "That's Percival. And he's up to no good. His talk is as smooth as ice, but his heart is as black as coal. Let's ignore him and maybe he'll leave us alone."

Percival shifted his stance. If he was agitated by Esperanza's words, he tried not to show it. With a twist of his head and a blink of his eyes, he quickly cast off his hostile mood like a snake shedding his skin. "Don't listen to her. You don't need her," he smiled as he tapped Esperanza's hand away and cupped Mai-Lyn's chin. He looked directly into her eyes. "You don't need anyone. I can see your strength, my dear. It's very attractive." He looked her up and down. "Yes, very attractive indeed. These two weaklings with you can't appreciate your potential." He looped his arm through Mai-Lyn's, gripping her forearm with his strong fist. "But I can. Let's head back out of the cave now. I'll keep you covered."

Mai-Lyn's body looked limp, almost deflated. Percival put his arm around Mai-Lyn's waist to guide her, but also to possess her. The two of them turned to exit the cave.

Esperanza felt panic rise inside her like lava ascending inside a volcano. She didn't trust Percival one bit and wanted to stop Mai-Lyn from what she was sure would be a huge mistake. But who was she to decide what was best for Mai-Lyn? Maybe she should just keep quiet. Yet she was relishing being with her two new friends. She already knew that she was stronger—thanks to being part of a tribe and being united with them in their joint quest. When she was weak, they strengthened her. And she sensed that they needed her too. Before this journey, she had always felt different from others in the village. She had considered herself independent and self-sufficient, even though deep inside, she had questioned herself. Now, seeing Mai-Lyn leaving with Percival, she felt as if a part of her was being ripped away. Oh, what to do?

Remember to listen for the water.

The water! Yes, that was it! The water would lead her. But where? And how? She closed her eyes, took a deep breath, and again heard the *plink, plink, plink* of the drops. The puddles softened the sound as the water gathered together from tiny trickles into a small stream. Where would it lead?

Esperanza looked down into the puddle and saw her reflection. Despite the smudge on her cheek, she looked different—wiser maybe? Before she looked away, she saw the smiling face of the old beggar from the woods looking over her shoulder. She blinked and spun around, but he was gone. She saw no trace that he had been there, yet she felt a new confidence deep within, as if he had left it for her as a gift. "Mai-Lyn! Stop!" Esperanza yelled. "Please, let's talk for a moment before you go."

When Mai-Lyn turned to look at her, Esperanza saw her glazed eyes and a new vague countenance. She must hurry! Percival surreptitiously edged Mai-Lyn closer to the cave entrance, but he couldn't turn her away from Esperanza.

"I couldn't bear it if you left us now. When I first saw you and Sienna at the well, my heart sank. I wanted to go on the dream journey alone. I was told I'd find everything I needed at the well. What I didn't know then was that you and Sienna *are* what I needed! And we are what *you* need. We may be different from each other, but we can't part ways now."

"Ha!" Percival grunted. "Such blather! Save the cheap talk for someone else!"

With a tear sliding down her cheek, Sienna

spoke with a strength that surprised everyone. "Mai-Lyn, my friend, don't be deceived. Percival said you don't need anyone, but that's just not true. I saw the look in your eyes when you brought us the helmet, the joy you wanted to share. What if you had your greatest moment and there was no one to share it with you? How hollow would that be? What if you hurt deep inside and there was no one to come alongside and carry your burden with you? We were made to be together."

"Idiotic drivel!" Percival cried as he tried to move Mai-Lyn, who was frozen like a statue.

Sienna looked down but continued on, now rubbing one hand along the sleeve covering her scarred forearm, gently kneading the skin underneath. "For a long time, I thought I never needed anyone else. I had my books and tried to convince myself that I didn't need people, that I didn't need friends. I never asked for help or accepted it if offered, which it rarely was. But what this journey with you has taught me is that we are better together." She looked at Mai-

Lyn, then Esperanza. "You are my sisters now. Like you said, Esperanza, we are different. But that's what makes this friendship so beautiful. Like a beautiful mosaic of broken pieces, when we came together, we became connected in a way that made each of us better." Sienna's voice caught in her throat as her emotions welled up.

Percival tried harder to move Mai-Lyn toward the exit, but she was now glued to the cavern floor. Short of picking her up and throwing her over his shoulder, there was nothing he could do.

"Mai-Lyn, oh Mai-Lyn!" Esperanza grasped for a pearl of wisdom, and from the recesses of her mind, Prudence's words floated to the surface.

"The king! He is close to us! Can you feel him near you? And he is a true promise-keeper! He knows your strengths, and your weaknesses too, and he loves *all* of you! We've come so far, my friend. Please! Don't abandon our journey now." She closed her eyes, raised one arm, and boldly declared the holy words she'd heard from Prudence. She said them aloud as much for herself as for her friends,

'The king watches over all who love him, but all the wicked he will destroy."[3]

Mai-Lyn blinked and shook her body.

"The Lord is near to all who call on Him. He is faithful in all he does."[4]

At that, Mai-Lyn broke away from Percival, his snakelike grip rendered powerless against the words Esperanza spoke.

With arms outstretched, Mai-Lyn ran to her companions and dropped like a crumpled heap at their feet. The other two knelt down, and the three girls hugged tightly, tears on every cheek.

"I'm so sorry," Mai-Lyn began. But the girls stopped her. There was no need to explain. With the unspoken understanding of the pressure on them to be able to go it alone in their world, they now saw it for the deception it was.

Percival slithered away, but Esperanza knew she had only won a battle, not the war.

The trio went deeper into the cave. Though they

lost the light from the cave entrance, slender beams glowing through tiny cracks above led their way. One of the beams lit upon a gleaming object beside a rock in the cave wall. Sienna spotted it first and cautiously approached the glowing article. As they all drew closer, their curiosity turned to amazement when they discovered a golden metal shield. *What sort of knight would leave his shield in a cave? Or his helmet in a tree, for that matter?* wondered Esperanza.

From the size and thickness of the shield, Esperanza was certain it was too heavy to lift. But with the first touch, the shield practically lifted itself. No sooner had they lifted the shield when they spied a large fissure in the cave wall providing an opening out of the cave. Dare they attempt to go back out into the storm with its piercing hailstones assaulting them at every turn? They would have to if they wanted to continue on their journey. But fear of the tempest kept them in the cave. They continued on in darkness, stumbling over stones.

When they eventually came to a flat stone wall,

they realized that not only was this the end of the cave, but that the stream of water had dried up. They'd left it back where they found the shield. With no other choice, they retraced their steps to the opening near where the shield had been. Using their new piece of armor to protect them from the storm's assault, the trio ventured forth out through the fissure into the squall.

Remarkably, under the safety of the shield, they stayed dry and unscathed. The hailstones that had held such power to harm them no longer bothered them. And because they were going through the storm rather than trying to evade it, they grew stronger with each step. They felt the thrill of victory as they journeyed forth—victory over the elements, but also victory over the lies and torment they'd previously endured.

Esperanza thought she heard laughter in the distance, but dismissed it as an illusion. It was probably just the whistle of the winds. The storm lost its power and slowly diminished to nothing as the girls, now carrying helmet and shield in their sacks, continued along the path. The sun broke through the dark clouds above and trees below, sparkling brightly in the drops on the leaves. The girls raced through the sunbeams. Sensing that the garden was within their reach, Esperanza's pace picked up and the other girls matched her step until they were practically dancing through the woods. Animals scattered out of their way as the trio approached, much like animals do before an approaching tsunami.

And perhaps those animal instincts were right.

7

The Battle

Before long, the sky grew dark, and Percival appeared again, this time astride an enormous, gleaming, jet-black horse. And he wasn't alone. He had brought a band of villagers with him. Some carried lanterns; others carried weapons.

"Well I see you are determined to continue on this preposterous expedition of yours. What fools you are! For your own good, your journey stops here."

Percival and his village henchmen blocked the

girls' path and began to surround them. The flames in the lanterns cast eerie shadows on their faces. The smoke from their torches burned the girls' eyes.

Oh, what was it Prudence said would help me in my time of need? Esperanza closed her eyes and tried to remember. "*The king grants the desires of those who fear him... he hears their cries for help and rescues them.*'"[5] *The king? Where is he? How can he possibly hear my cry for help? How can he rescue me and my friends? Dare I trust these words? But what other choice do I have now?* Barely moving her lips, Esperanza began to speak to the magical king that Prudence seemed to know personally.

"I'm not sure if you can hear me or see me, but I—I mean *we*—need help. Please, oh king, please rescue us."

The words had barely left her lips when the leaves began to flutter, as if a strong wind was blowing through them. The thunderous sound of horse's hooves intensified as a mysterious rider raced toward the terrifying circle around them. To their astonishment, a knight straddling an alabaster white horse approached. The knight sat high in his saddle wearing brilliant, polished armor from neck to toe—a golden breastplate, chainmail chausses on his legs, and a dazzling sword—which he raised high above his head. He entered the semicircle to address Percival face-to-face.

"So we meet again, Percival."

Percival glowered at his opponent. "Yes, once again we meet. Don't you have anything better to do than rescue insignificant damsels in distress?"

"Actually, no, I do not. Rescue is my paramount purpose."

"Well, unfortunately, you're too late. You are just one knight on a single horse. You will not be able to defeat all of us."

The villagers murmured and kept their eyes down, all the while trembling and refusing to look at the knight.

"This is between you and me, Percival. Leave them out of it," said the knight.

"You'd like that, wouldn't you?" sneered Percival. "Well, they are mine and will do as I bid. You will *not* be able to defeat us!"

"Like my father defeated you?" The knight didn't even raise his voice, but the force behind it was felt.

"Ha! Your father!" Percival spat on the ground. "Your father is selfish, wanting all the glory for himself. Look around—these people, his people, are *my* people now! And they always will be! I will *never* let them return to him!"

Esperanza and Sienna shook with terror. Mai-Lyn scowled and stood taller with each word Percival spoke. She seemed ready to enter the battle herself. Only her shaking knees gave an indication of the panic she must have felt.

The knight looked at the girls with compassion. "Fear not, beloved. There are more that are with us than are with them."[6]

Percival laughed. "You're daft!"

The knight smiled. "Look around. You will see

that I am not alone. I am never alone."

Slowly, Percival's eyes moved from the knight to the trees, then up to the treetops covering them. Fear began to register across his face. Esperanza turned and looked up at the branches circled overhead too.

Hundreds of pairs of eyes filled the treetops. Through the dark leaves, round, white eagle eyes barely blinked, and yellow catlike eyes stared at Percival and his minions. There must have been every kind of fierce creature hiding within the foliage, waiting for the moment to be summoned into action. Above the treetops, like a vast crowd of witnesses, clouds moved in formations, appearing to float in unison.

Percival's eyes narrowed, and his shoulders straightened. He raised his sword, pointed it forward, dug his heels into his horse's flanks, and charged at the knight. The knight pulled his horse's reins to easily sidestep Percival's attack. He raised his sword high and circled it above his head. The sword emanated light like the sun. That seemed to anger

Percival even more. He turned his horse around and charged back again toward the knight.

The knight did not turn around. He stood high in his stirrups and shouted, "I died once for these. I will not die again!" He waved the glowing sword toward the villagers, who stumbled and dropped to the ground. They cried out in distress and held their hands to their eyes.

As Percival's horse neared, the knight spun around and pointed the glowing sword directly at Percival, who fell backwards off his horse. Percival rolled and quickly jumped to his feet. He held his sword high, leveled it at the knight, and ran toward him. The knight slid off his horse to confront Percival head on. Facing each other, they circled around. Swords clashed in a deathly dance. Percival jabbed over and over. The glowing sword deflected each jab. The girls stood motionless, like petrified statues, as their rescuer fought on their behalf.

The leaves above fluttered as wings flapped. Growls and squawks rose in intensity. The animals readied themselves to engage in the fight below, just waiting for the signal from their commander.

Percival spiked the tip of his sword into the ground and used it to vault over the knight to attack him from behind. The knight whirled around to face Percival and placed his feet securely in a defensive stance. He extended his arms, the gleaming sword level with one hand on either end. As Percival rushed at him, the knight let go of the tip of the sword and the point swung straight toward Percival's heart.

Percival swerved, and the sword tip caught his arm, slicing deep into the flesh. He stumbled and fell to one knee, his good hand covering his bloody bicep. Percival turned his head and whistled. As the black horse trotted toward his master, Percival raised himself up and sprinted toward him.

"Percival, today you suffer a defeat in battle, but one day you will be vanquished forever. The next time we meet, I will crush your head, and you will no longer torment my people."

Percival grabbed the reins with his good arm and

swung up to the saddle. With one arm limp at his side, momentum took him too far over the top. Falling over the other side, his foot caught in the stirrup, and the horse raced off with Percival dragging along the ground.

The girls gaped as the ebony horse hauled Percival across the clearing and into the dark forest, taking him away from both the village behind them and the garden trail before them. The sun emerged from the darkness, and the knight turned to look at the blinded villagers with compassion. They were like sheep without a shepherd.[7]

"Stand up!"

The villagers slowly rose to their feet. They shook their heads, their eyes cloudy with vacant stares.

The knight pulled a rope out of his saddlebag. Tapping one of the stronger men on the shoulder, the knight handed him one end of the rope and instructed him to pass it along to the next man and so on, until all the villagers had one hand on the rope and one hand holding their lanterns. The knight grabbed the other end of the rope and climbed upon his horse. He gently spurred the horse's flanks and slowly began to lead the entire company of men back toward the village.

The knight glanced at the girls as he departed from them. "Carry on." He pointed his sword eastward toward the path out of the forest glen. "Your journey continues."

There was something familiar about the knight, but Esperanza wasn't sure what it was. Had she encountered him before? No, of course not. That would be ridiculous. When had a common girl like her ever seen a knight? Still, his eyes glowed with a familiar compassion, and that voice—equally powerful and kind. Had she heard it before? She shook her head. *An ordinary girl like me needn't entertain such fanciful thoughts.*

With the battle behind them, the trio set out once again toward the magical garden, this time with a new confidence. Their mysterious rescuer was no longer in sight, but Esperanza felt certain they'd see him again.

The sound of rushing water got louder with each step, so loud it almost drowned out the birds, who were chirping and singing to their hearts' content. Almost, but not quite. The songs of the birds echoed through the forest as flocks flew in unison from treetop to treetop and back again.

Bushes lined both sides of the trail. Sienna peeked between them.

"Oh look! The rabbits and foxes are playing together in the clearing."

"How odd!" Esperanza said. "That would never happen in the village. Both animals and people distrust anyone who is the least bit different from them."

Esperanza moved with a grace she didn't know she had. She was sure that the garden was near. Maybe one more bend in the path? For as long as she could remember, the garden had been a mystery—a legend. She didn't know if it was true, but she wholeheartedly wished it was. It held a promise that one day she could escape the oppression of the village. And now . . . now it might be within her reach!

Or maybe not.

8

The Waterfall

A ***s the trio rounded the next bend,*** a waterfall came into view. The white rushing water cascaded from high atop a mountain. The sunshine sparkled brightly, and a lovely rainbow in the spray beckoned them to come closer. Invisible drops of water tickled their noses and sprinkled their arms; however, immediately before them, the path had ended abruptly. An uncrossable chasm lay straight ahead—a steep canyon so deep, they couldn't see the bottom.

Was our journey all a tease? Are we destined to

stay on this side forever? How could we have come this far, and gone through all we have, only to find ourselves in this impossible situation? Esperanza dropped down in the middle of the path, and tears that had welled up inside now overflowed like the waterfall across the chasm.

Remember the water. You have everything you need.

Those words seemed to mock Esperanza. The water, right there before her eyes, was totally unattainable. And everything she needed? Well, she had her friends, but what help were they to her now? They were trapped with her. Her shoulders shook with uncontrollable sobs. She had never felt so hopeless. *It was better before—when the garden was just a dream, a fantasy.* But now, seeing it almost within her reach, but unable to get there, was just too much to bear.

Mai-Lyn and Sienna sat down beside her. They put their arms on Esperanza's shoulders. "I don't have any words," Mai-Lyn whispered. "I wish I knew what to say, but I'm so disappointed too." With hopes dashed and no plan in sight, Sienna started singing.

"*I will exalt you, my king,*" Sienna began. "*I will praise your name forever and ever.*"

Esperanza raised her head at hearing Prudence's song in Sienna's sweet, young voice. Sienna continued, "*The king is close to all who call on him, yes, to all who call on him in truth.*

"*The king helps the fallen and lifts those bent beneath their loads. I will praise the king, and may everyone on earth praise him forever and ever.*"[8]

The words reached a place deep inside Esperanza's broken heart. *Does the king hear my cries? Could he, would he rescue me now? Now that I am in such despair? How can he?*

Hearing the crunch of footsteps on the path, she turned around. The beggar she had seen in the maze of trees, with the face she had seen reflected in the puddle, stood before her. His body was bowed and gnarled, but his eyes shone like the noon sun. Who was this man, and why did they see him at the most difficult times of their journey?

"My dears, would you like me to help you cross this chasm?" Esperanza thought she recognized his voice, but from where? He was a most unlikely hero. He looked far too feeble and frail to help them. And could he be trusted? *But what choice do we have? Do we go with the beggar or return to the village in shame?* Neither option seemed possible. But there was something familiar about him—something in his eyes, something that began to reassure her. Perhaps he could help them. Or maybe they and their youthful strength could help him in some way.

"Yes, sir. We do need help. We've come so far. I can't imagine what you can possibly do, but if you say you can help, I will believe you."

The old beggar smiled, just like he had in the forest and the cave. He nodded his approval at her trust in him. "Then please hand me your helmet and shield."

"But sir," she whispered, "we found these on our journey. We need them. You are asking us to surrender the most valuable things we have, the only things we have."

"I understand. Nevertheless, I'm asking you to trust me. I can take you across the chasm, but I will need you to surrender what you think are your treasures. For holding too tightly to what you cherish can keep you from what is truly valuable."

The girls looked at each other. Esperanza pondered his words. What a most unusual request. Did they dare to relinquish what they held so dear and trust this stranger, one who held out a mere scrap of hope? Could they put their confidence in this improbable rescuer? And what did a beggar need with a helmet and shield anyway? Yet, despite how the helmet and shield had helped them thus far, they wouldn't be any use in helping the girls cross the chasm. And if the beggar was telling the truth, they needed to trust him. Together, the girls held out their arms, offering their treasures to the beggar.

Again with a smile, the beggar nodded and took the prizes.

A soft wind began to swirl around him. As they stared wide-eyed, the hood that covered his snow-white hair fell back. His burlap cloak lifted away from his body as he raised his staff to the sky. Soon all the girls could see was a spinning, dusty, brown cloud. When the spinning finally stopped, the girls blinked. Before them stood the shining knight who had rescued them in the battle. From beneath his helmet shone the beggar's caring eyes. His raised arm held the powerful, glowing sword; his other arm bore the golden shield.

"Be not discouraged, my friends. I have given you everything you need. Everything. Even a way to cross this chasm. You see, I have gone before you. I have descended the depths and ascended the other side. I will take you. You will see that there is no valley so deep that I cannot descend deeper still. Or a mountain so high that I cannot ascend." Mai-Lyn and Sienna looked at Esperanza. "We've come this far," she whispered.

"Come, my dears. Let me show you the way."

The voice! It was the voice she had heard in her dream. The voice that told her, "My dear Esperanza, listen for the water. I have given you everything you need at the well." He had indeed given her everything she needed—at the well, in the forest, through the labyrinth, in the cave, during the battle. There was never a moment that she had lacked for anything, although at the time she'd thought she did. And now here he was at the precipice, about to lead them to the garden and the waterfall—the source of life.

"Come, let's draw close to the edge. Do not be afraid. I will not leave you or forsake you."

With equal amounts of terror and trust, Esperanza inched closer to the edge with Mai-Lyn and Sienna on each side. As they did, the knight stretched out his arm toward the waterfall. They saw something glimmer over the great gorge. Like a gossamer web glistening in the sun, it was barely visible. But the closer they got, they realized they were seeing a translucent and ethereal footbridge. *Had it been there all along*? They couldn't be sure.

Cautiously, they stepped out onto the bridge and crossed the chasm, firmly supported by their knight. Once on the other side, they sprinted all the way to the base of the waterfall. The knight preceded them and invited them one by one to dance with him and then to step into the azure pool.

Mai-Lyn went first, eager to dip into the cleansing pool, her countenance beaming, the guilt she'd said plagued her seemingly washed away with each step. Sienna followed, and soon Esperanza did too. Each girl danced with her hero, the praise coming from her friends echoed what Esperanza felt inside. They were renewed in spirit and freed from fear.

The touch of the water on their skin brought a healing to their souls. They felt the cool liquid on the outside, but their hearts burned on the inside. Radiating from their hearts, a warmth filled them to the top of their heads and the tips of their toes. Their guilt and shame dissipated, washed away in the cleansing waters.

As they immersed themselves deeper into the water, their drab, sullied clothes transformed into gleaming new garments of turquoise, lapis, and teal. The new garments served as an outward reflection of their inward transformations. The journey had changed them. No longer uncertain or suspicious, they shared a freedom and friendship that knit them together.

They thought they could stay there forever. But that was not to be.

9

The Garden

"It's time." The knight spoke, breaking through their enchantment.

"Time, sir?" Esperanza asked. "Time for what?"

"It's time to go."

"Oh no!" Esperanza gasped. "Please don't make us leave. I can't bear to leave this place. I'm afraid to lose the joy I feel."

"My dear, do you trust me?" The knight's beautiful eyes looked straight into hers.

Esperanza's fear left immediately. "Of course, I

trust you. How could I not? To whom else would I go?"[9]

He looked at the three girls. "I am taking you all to meet someone."

"Meet someone?" asked Sienna.

"Yes, to meet someone. Come, let us go this way. It's time to climb." Their knight led them out from the pool and up a slippery, rocky path. The sound of the waterfall amplified with each cautious step. The mist glistened on their new garments.

They continued up the path, then around a bend and through what looked like the entrance to a tunnel. The flow of the water now became a deafening roar. To their surprise, the tunnel was not a tunnel at all! It turned out to be the entrance to a grotto behind the waterfall. They ran into the grotto and danced around, arms raised high as the mist inside the cavern sparkled upon them like glitter.

"Look out there. What do you see?" The knight pointed through the curtain of pounding water.

"There's the green of the treetops shimmering in

the sun." Mai-Lyn cried out and pointed through the flume of water. "That's where I climbed up the tree limbs in the forest and first glimpsed the garden."

Sienna pointed. "Oh, there's something brown moving over there. Maybe it's a deer and her babes scampering over the hedges." Of course, Sienna would notice the animals.

"I see the blue of the pool where we danced, and the colors of the flowers along the path." Esperanza said, cherishing the memory of the moment her shame and fear washed away.

"You each see many things that you've seen before. But look again; do you see them clearly?"

The girls squinted, peering out through the cascade of water, looking out to the garden and beyond. They had to agree. Though they could discern the places they'd been, they could not see any of them clearly.

"This is how it is when you live in the village. My father and I created all that you see, and you were meant to enjoy it. But when you dwell across the chasm, what you see around you is a poor reflection of what I intended. The lies and deceptions create a veiled view of what truth is. What you think is love is at best a deep friendship, and at worst an exploitive relationship. It differs greatly from the sacrificial love that my Father and I know and have for you.

"Come this way now. We're going to meet my father, the king." The knight led them out of the grotto and on a steep path up the mountain to the top of the waterfall. The climb would have been exhausting if they had been anywhere else. But here in this garden, knowing that they were on their way to meet the king, their steps practically soared.

The top of the mountain was level, and it seemed they could see for miles in every direction. Across the summit, they saw a glow—as if the sun were rising from that very spot. The light radiated as far as their eyes could see. A river flowed from the sunrise point, down the waterfall, and through the rest of the garden. Beside the river, animals picnicked under an enormous tree laden with life-giving fruit. And beyond the garden, they could almost make out walls made of translucent gemstones—sapphires, amethysts, and emeralds. They turned back toward their knight, who led them on toward the sunrise. "This is the way," he said.

As they neared the light, a gleaming throne appeared. The throne, made of luminous gold, seemed to emit its own light, the source of the glow from across the plateau. Engraved in the golden throne were images of a lion and an eagle.

Seated on the throne, the king beckoned them closer. "Welcome, my daughters. I see you have met my dearly loved son who brings me great joy."[10] The king smiled, and the light shone even brighter, if that were possible. The knight sat down beside his father's right hand.

Despite her joy, Esperanza felt bewildered. The knight was the king's son, yet the king called them his daughters. Perceiving her confusion, the king asked, "My dear, do you know what it means to be my child?"

Esperanza hesitated, not wanting to seem ungrateful to the king, yet not comprehending what he meant. "I'm not sure exactly," she replied honestly, which she figured was the best way to start a relationship.

"When you are my child, you are secure in my love. Our connection is for a lifetime. You will grow and mature, and our relationship will deepen with understanding and compassion. Today is just the beginning of a new life in which you experience my limitless love.[11] As your father, I will protect you and teach you in the ways you should go."

Esperanza sighed, both from exhilaration and exhaustion.

The king smiled gently. "You have come a long way."

"Yes, Your Majesty. We have traveled far, and we learned so much along the way. But now, here in this place, we feel as if our journey has just begun."

"I'm glad you feel that way," said the king, "for there is yet much ahead of you."

"We are your handmaidens, sir. We want to serve you well."[12]

"Then you will return to the village." His words sounded final.

Sienna and Mai-Lyn gasped. Esperanza pleaded. "Oh, Your Majesty, must we? The village is so dark and dismal. After seeing the beauty of the garden, we want to stay here forever."

"I understand. And you will come back at the proper time. But now, you must share the good news of this place with those who don't remember it." The king looked wistfully out beyond the walls. A trace of sadness crossed his face. "To all who are thirsty, I will give freely from the springs of the water of life. But how will they believe if they have never heard? They must be told." He turned to the girls and smiled.

Esperanza took a deep breath then exhaled. The king was right. She glanced at the other girls and they nodded. "We understand, Your Majesty. If the villagers could know what we now know, how different their lives would be."

"Then you must tell them. When they see your

transformation, they will want to know." He pointed to the side of the throne. "I have a gift for each of you for the journey back."

The king and the knight stood. Beside the throne sat three pairs of beautiful golden slippers. The girls tried them on, and remarkably, each pair of shoes fit each pair of feet perfectly. "How beautiful are the feet of those who bring the good news,"[13] the king smiled as the girls departed.

The trio felt a new peace deep in their souls that permeated their whole beings. That peace supplied them with the confidence they would need to share the good news of their journey, their audacious adventures with their knight, and the glorious meeting with their king.

Would this peace last long enough to give them the strength they needed to return to the village and relate their story to those still in darkness?

10

The Return

Not quite sure of the way back, the trio decided to follow the river. The water had led them this far; surely it would continue to direct them.

Beside the river, golden sunflowers raised their heads as violet irises stretched up to the sun. The scent of roses filled their noses. Unexpectedly, the path along the river did not lead the trio to the footbridge by which they had come. Instead, they arrived at soaring jeweled parapets that surrounded the garden. The gemstones adorning the walls gleamed in the sunlight, reflecting every color of the rainbow from the foundation to the top. The reflections played lights and shadows on the girls' faces, arms, and clothing, eliciting delighted squeals.

"This can't be the end of the path," Mai-Lyn stepped back, and her eyes scoured the wall for an exit. "The river continues under the wall, but we can't go that way."

The girls walked along the jeweled wall until they arrived at an enormous, luminescent pearl entrance. A flaming sword glowed above the gateway, and on either side stood a pair of winged guards. Nodding to the trio, one duo opened wide the pearlescent gates. Thanking the guards, the girls walked along a flower-strewn path, and soon the trail met the river providing their return route to the village.

Before long, before the colors started to dim as the village came into view. Surprisingly, the journey home seemed much shorter. But doesn't the trip home always seem shorter. As they neared the village, they spotted Prudence waiting for them at her garden gate. Despite leaning on her cane, Prudence seemed younger, her skin more vibrant. All three girls sprinted to greet her.

"So tell me, dears. Was the garden everything you hoped it would be? And the King . . ." Her eyes misted with emotion. "How is our beloved King?"

All three girls started speaking at once.

Prudence laughed. "Come inside for a moment before you go on to the village square. Let's have some sweet tea, and you can tell me about your journey."

Esperanza opened the heavy wooden door, and the girls raced in. Prudence made herself comfortable in her big cozy chair, and the girls nestled at her feet after making the tea. Esperanza laid her head against Prudence's knees while Mai-Lyn recounted their journey through the maze of trees and seeing the garden from afar. When Sienna told of their adventure in the cave, Mai-Lyn looked down and shook her head. "It's so easy to be deceived. I felt so ashamed, but the King and the knight loved me just the same as if I'd never gone with Percival."

After the girls narrated their tales of the battle, the waterfall, and meeting the beggar, the knight, and the King, Esperanza turned and kneeled to face Prudence. "Prudence, why didn't you ever tell me the story? The villagers talk in whispers and pretend the garden isn't real. You knew and kept it a secret from me until now. I don't understand."

"Ah, my child. It was so hard for me not to share the glorious truth with you. But you weren't ready to receive it. A mama doesn't give a valuable treasure to her baby, for the youngster could trample it. The babe can't appreciate its worth. So I waited, and each day I prayed for the time that the treasure would be yours. To see you three now was worth the wait. I'm grateful to have lived long enough to experience this joy."

She pointed, palms up, to the door. "There is a village full of people who need to share in this too. They need to be awakened from the slumber that

Percival cast over them. It's their time now."

Esperanza's thoughts raced. "But what will we say? How will they receive our testimony?"

Prudence pointed to the gold-edged book, and Sienna brought it over. She ran her hands over the cover and held it close to her chest. "I've never seen a book so beautiful." Sienna said. "And I've seen many books!"

Prudence took the book, opened the front cover, and flipped through the pages. "This is more than just a book with words on paper pages. This book is like the river that quenches thirst and washes us clean. It is a love letter from our king. Like a magic mirror in the fairy tales, the book is a way to "see" the king. He speaks to us through these words—words of encouragement, teaching, and discipline. The book tells our story—our history. And it contains many songs too!"

Sienna's face lit up. "Songs?"

Prudence patted her hand. "The book not only nourishes our soul and feeds our spirit; it works like a map leading us in the way we should go.

"And now, my dears, you should go. There are people that need to hear your story. Because of the dark times you have been through, you are able to reach them in their dark places. And to share the joy that comes in the morning."

Esperanza reached for the book. "We'll treasure it."

"But first . . .," Prudence smiled, and the tears on her cheek this time were tears of happiness. "…ladies, let's enjoy our tea and soup."

11

The Testimony

A***fter the girls ate their fill,*** they bade Prudence farewell. They brought the book of truth with them as they made their way back to the center of the village.

Was the village really always this dark? Esperanza once again heard the familiar *clip, clip, clip* of her shoes on the hard stone path. *What will we say? Will we be able to break through to them? Oh King, please lead us. Please give us the right words.*

"Look over there." Sienna pointed to the riverbed beside the path along their walk into town.

The river, which had dried up long ago, now displayed trickles of water dribbling through it.

Well that's interesting.

As they neared the village gate, dusty children stopped their game of tossing rocks. They stared at the trio as they approached. One by one, each rock dropped with a soft thud to the ground. A little girl turned and ran.

"Mama! Come look! Hurry! The girls are bringing us light!"

The trio stopped and looked at each other. Their faces possessed a new radiance, and a glow of light trailed behind each of them. With each movement they made, the light swayed with the grace of a ballerina. *Would their joy never end?*

The girls swung wide the village gate with renewed confidence. They looked around the village center with fresh eyes. They noticed the people hiding in the shadows and felt compassion instead of apprehension.

The little girl pulled her mama, Mrs. Baker,

toward the trio.

"Not now, Millie. I need to deliver this bread to the tavern."

"Mrs. Baker, can I walk with you to the tavern? I so love your bread." Esperanza smiled, grateful for the opportunity to speak with the creator of her favored indulgence.

Mrs. Baker smoothed her dingy apron and cautiously peeked at her favorite customer.

"Esperanza, you look different."

"Yes, I *am* different, Mrs. Baker! I've just returned from the garden after meeting the King. I have so much to share with you."

Mrs. Baker frowned. "The garden? But that's just a legend . . . isn't it?"

"No, Mrs. Baker. It's true; it's all true. We spoke with the King and his son, the knight. They are wise and kind." She looked at the baker's weary eyes and added. "And they love you completely."

Mrs. Baker turned her head, averting her eyes.

Esperanza pointed to Mai-Lyn and Sienna. "My

friends and I went on a miraculous journey. All the lies and deceptions we believed here in the village were washed away in the pool of our transformation. We can see clearly for the first time."

"Esperanza, of course the king loves you and your friends. You are beautiful girls. I'm plain and plump. And flustered all the time." She looked down at her daughter, still enraptured, staring at the girls while tugging at her mom's apron. "Millie, go play with the children."

"But Mama! I don't want to."

Mrs. Baker sighed. She looked back at Esperanza. "There's nothing special about me. I certainly wouldn't want to take up a king's time." Before Esperanza could reply, she added, "And if there is a king, why are things so bleak around here?"

Esperanza reached out and touched the lady's arm. "Oh, Mrs. Baker, there's so much I don't know. I'm still learning. But what I do know is that the king is good, so very good, and full of love. People here are deceived. We never knew, but we have a choice.

We can choose whether to follow the King or the deceiver. The King doesn't see you as plain or plump. He sees you as he made you—precious and prized. He is a glorious creator. He made you, and nothing he makes is inferior."

Mrs. Baker looked down. She slowly shook her head.

"Mrs. Baker, please! See that book?" She pointed to Sienna, who held the treasured book. "It is full of letters written by the king! It tells me, and you, that we are wonderfully made!"

Sienna walked over to Esperanza and the two bakers and displayed the book in her outstretched arms. "Mrs. Baker, this book is different from other books. The words in it give life."

Mrs. Baker looked up at the girls. A tear welled in her eye. "I would like to believe that what you say is true. For me . . . and for my children."

Sienna's face shone. "Mrs. Baker, may I take Millie with me for a moment?"

"Yes, I'm sure she would love to go with you."

Sienna took Millie's hand. "Hi Millie! Would you like to go with me to the bookstore over there? I would like to show this book of truth to my friend, the shop owner."

Millie jumped up and down, raising both her arms, barely containing her excitement.

As Sienna and Millie crossed the village center, Mai-Lyn meandered across the square toward the blacksmith's shop.

When Mrs. Baker entered the tavern, she took the bread from Esperanza. "Thank you for walking with me, Esperanza. I will think about what you said."

"Yes, Mrs. Baker! Please do! I'm sure you'll see the light of truth, as we have." Esperanza turned away from the tavern to see Mai-Lyn standing by the wide-open entrance to the blacksmith's barn. She walked across the square. "Mai-Lyn, why are you standing here?"

Mai-Lyn turned toward Esperanza, her eyes glassy with tears. "See that boy in there? I saw him at the well before we left on our journey."

Esperanza looked into barn for a better view of the blacksmith's workspace. Halfway down the right wall—in the middle of shop—a white-hot forge stood beside a heavy wooden bench sporting a variety of black iron tools, tongs, and jigs. On the left wall, horses were nestled in stalls that lined the side of the barn. To the left, a young man combed the mane of a small palomino horse.

"Easy there, Spirit. Mr. Smith will be back soon to fix that pebble in your shoe."

A tear spilled down Mai-Lyn's cheeks.

Esperanza put her arm across Mai-Lyn's shoulder. "What is it, my friend?"

"Do you smell anything?"

Esperanza sniffed, "Well, there's hay and manure. Hmmm . . . also sweat and something burning."

"When I was waiting at the well before you and Sienna arrived, I saw this boy. He was getting buckets of water for the horses. I could have helped him. But I didn't. I moved away from him. I didn't like his smell. Or his clothes. Ha! As if mine were any better. I held my nose and looked at him like he was dirt beneath my feet, because I thought he was." She wiped another tear away. "I'm so ashamed now. He annoyed me. Why, everybody annoyed me! When I think of all the people I treated so badly, I don't know if I can face them."

Esperanza faced her friend. "Mai-Lyn, that's who you *were,* not who you *are.* Remember—the king called us his daughters, deeply loved and forgiven."

Micah looked up and saw the two girls at the entrance to his shop. "Can I help you?" He walked out to greet them.

"Do you remember me?" asked Mai-Lyn quietly.

A wave of recognition swept over him as he squinted at Mai-Lyn. His eyes turned away, but he quickly looked back. "You look different."

"Yes, I am different. I want to tell you how sorry I am for acting the way I did at the well."

Micah nodded and turned to Esperanza. "Who

are you?"

"My name is Esperanza. Mai-Lyn and I have just returned from a journey to the garden where we met the king."

"The garden? So the legend is true?" Micah looked from one girl to the other and back again. "Mr. Smith said his grandfather believed it. He might have even been to the garden himself. But Mr. Smith says it's nonsense to believe in fairytales. He listens to whatever Percival says."

"Percival is a liar and a deceiver! We've been to the garden and spoken with the king." Esperanza extended her hands. "And with our own eyes, we've seen the knight defeat Percival in battle."

Micah stared directly at Esperanza. "Esperanza means hope, doesn't it?"

Now it was Esperanza's turn to tear up. "Yes, hope. I was . . . *we were* . . . lost souls here in the village. Breathing, moving, talking, but dead inside. But I heard whispers about a magical garden and a king who lived there. I never lost hope that one day I would discover this to be true. And it is!" Esperanza looked more intently at this young man before her. "And what is your name?"

"I'm Micah. I want to believe what you say about the garden. And the king. I just don't know. It's so dark here. But there's something about you that makes me want to know more."

As he spoke, Sienna and Millie came out of the bookseller shop. Millie ran ahead of Sienna to hug Esperanza around her knees. As Sienna crossed the square, villagers emerged from the shadows in the corners. Their zombie faces and tattered gray clothing brought a chill to the air, and Sienna picked up her speed toward the blacksmith shop. The villagers kept coming.

"Wait!" shouted a tall man on the edge of the group. "You were the girls in the forest clearing, weren't you?"

Esperanza, Sienna, and Mai-Lyn stared at the villagers, their feet glued to the cobblestones. Millie hid behind their skirts. Micah came around the villagers to stand in front of the girls.

The villagers stretched out their arms and called again to the trio as they began walking away. “You! Wait!”

The village gate rattled, and a bloody and bruised Percival stepped through. He led his horse to the blacksmith shop and glared at the girls. “I will make you rue the day you ever stepped out of this village.”

Now it was Esperanza’s knees that rattled.

12

The Transformation

T***he villagers called out to the tall man on the end.*** "Henrick! Where are they?" "Do you see them, Henrick?"

"Yes, men! I see them. They are by Mr. Smith's shop."

"Lead us to them, Henrick!"

Esperanza felt her lungs tighten as she realized they were trapped. Percival blocked them on their left. The approaching villagers left no room for escape.

"WAIT there!" Henrick's voice boomed. "We want to talk to you."

Esperanza and the girls had no choice but to wait. As the villagers got closer, Esperanza could see the men's faces, their eyes cloudy and vacant. But the tall one, Henrick, appeared different. His blue eyes looked at the girls clearly. The men followed his directions. He brought the men to stand before the trio, then he knelt on one knee before the girls and instructed the blind men to do the same.

"*What* are you doing?!" Percival shouted. "Stand up, you idiots!"

Henrick bowed his head, then looked up at each of the girls. "I was blinded, but now I see." He cleared his throat. "At the battle in the forest, the knight blinded our eyes with the light of his sword. He led us back to the village, and the whole time we walked with him, he told us about his father and himself—and about ourselves. He did not condemn us. He asked where our accuser was and told us to live according to the truth—his truth. We felt warm inside when he was with us."

Esperanza felt that warmth too, both when she was with the knight, and now, hearing Henrick's testimony.

Percival had enough. He sputtered, and his voice nearly exploded with frustration. "What are you saying, man? It was *me!* I'm the one who has given you everything you wanted. *Me!* Not that power-hungry knight. Listen to what I've told you all your life, not that impostor!"

Henrick stood up, swiveled to face Percival, pointed his finger, and looked directly at him. *"You* are the imposter, Percival! You deceived us with your lies and half-truths. But everything has changed now. You are no longer welcome here in our village."

At that, something like scales fell from the other men's eyes. They looked around, stood up, and starting shouting with joy. "We can see again!" "No, we can see for the first time!"

Henrick looked at the girls. "The scales fell off my eyes when the knight gave me the rope and put his hand on my shoulder. We've been wondering when the others would be able to see again."

Percival stood taller and puffed his chest out like a blowfish trying to scare off an opponent. Arrogance oozed from his every pore. He opened his mouth to speak, but Mai-Lyn held up her hand, palm faced at Percival. *"No!* You have nothing more to say to us!"

Esperanza found her voice. She looked at Percival through narrowed eyes. "Percival, you act like a roaring lion, pacing to and fro around here, seeking whom you may devour. But you are a lion with your teeth knocked out. The knight has conquered you. You are pathetically desperate in your attempt to try to control us when you are a defeated foe!"

Percival's face turned red with rage. "Who are *you* to call *me* pathetic, you wretched little waif!"

"I am a daughter of the King! That's who I am! You have no power over me any longer."

Percival's demeanor immediately changed from haughty to frightened. Esperanza eyes grew wide, amazed at the power of her words to elicit this transformation.

"You heard the girl, Percival. You have no power here any longer. Get out of this village, and stay out!"

Esperanza wheeled around at the voice behind her. The knight stood tall behind the girls. It was *his* presence that had made Percival shrink like a bully who encountered the bigger, stronger brother of his victim.

Micah had been holding the reins to Percival's horse. "Here, Percival. Take your horse and go."

"Hmmph! What's going on here?" The village mayor approached the crowd in front of the blacksmith's shop.

"Ah, Percival. I see . . . Oh! Oh, my. Well, um . . . I see you look a bit worse for the wear."

"Most esteemed mayor, may we have a word?" Now Sienna found her voice. "You are influential here in this village, with great authority over your citizens. I hope that you will hear and accept our testimony about what we have experienced."

The mayor raised his chin up high and looked down at Sienna. "Ah, little one. So you have a testimony, do you?"

"Yes, sir, I do." As she spoke, the knight stepped out from behind the girls, out of the shadow of the blacksmith's shop.

The mayor's eyes widened. "And who is this?"

"This is our rescuer, Mr. Mayor. This knight has brought us out of the darkness into the light."

"Darkness, you say? Here in my village?"

As the mayor spoke, Mrs. Baker joined the crowd. She brought with her the tavern owner, along with all his patrons. The bookseller had peeked into the cobbler's and seamstress's shops and urged them to come join the growing crowd. Other villagers arrived from all corners of the square. Still more came from their homes beyond the village center.

In front of all his constituents, the mayor acquiesced to hear the testimonies, and not just from the girls, but from the men who had been in the forest. One by one, as the people shared their stories, light began to spread. The glow widened from the blacksmith's shop, across the well in the plaza, until it reached the village gate and beyond. The sky changed from cloudy gray to bright azure blue.

The testimonies produced cheers and laughter throughout the crowd. Some had never heard a laugh or seen a smile before.

No one noticed that Percival had disappeared.

Then the testimonies concluded. Esperanza called to the crowd, "Come! Let us plant flowers down by the dried riverbed. The garden is beautiful and so full of flowers. Perhaps if we plant flowers here, the river will flow again."

Some villagers disagreed. "Silly girl; flowers are frivolous. You can't eat flowers." But others agreed to try. So the large crowd paraded through the square, out the gate, and toward the dried-up riverbed. But when they got there, they were amazed. No longer did tiny rivulets trickle through the cracked river bottom. Now water rushed along, nearly overflowing its banks.

Strangely, the roar of the rushing river reminded the girls of the voice of the king.

Henrick ran to the river and jumped in. He plunged below the surface and then rose up out of the water like a salmon running upstream. He raised his arms and shouted with joy. He emerged from the river with a glow around his head, his clothes transformed. Another villager walked down to the riverbed, his pace increasing with each step closer to the water. Then another villager followed, and another. The sound of laughter rose from the rushing water. And before long, every villager was soaking wet in gleaming new garments.

Esperanza looked around. Behind her, at the village gate, she spotted the knight astride his horse. His eyes sparkled like the jewels in the garden walls, and his smile cast a warm radiance around him.

In the distance, down the road past Prudence's cottage, Esperanza saw what looked like the sunrise blazing from a flat-topped mountain, and she knew that the source of the waters flowing in the river came from that mountaintop.

She saw people working heartily for their king. Mr. and Mrs. Baker gathered their children. "Our blessings!" Even the mayor held a trowel and helped plant new seedlings.

Mr. Smith stood to the side, his head bowed. Micah placed a hand on his shoulder. Esperanza couldn't hear them, but she knew Micah was encouraging Mr. Smith that despite his previous refusal to accept the legend as true, the King would surely welcome him.

Micah glanced up and saw Esperanza looking his way. He broke into a smile that warmed her heart. Esperanza smiled back.

Was it ever this bright in the village?

About the Author

Susan is a Jewish Jersey girl who loves Jesus and by His grace is loved by Him. Susan is a wife who works with her rock star chiropractor husband by day and writes by night and mom of two future world-changers.

Her blog, Eternity Café, shares encouraging stories of everyday life that reflect the eternal truths of God which incite passion and purpose out of the mundane and ordinary. She writes and speaks to women's groups on this and a wide variety of topics, all designed to encourage, equip, and edify with enthusiasm for an eternal perspective.

She is also the co-founder and Executive Director of Justice Network which raises awareness about human trafficking and support for organizations locally and globally that are already on the front lines fighting this heinous evil.

www.susanpanzica.com

www.-justice-network.org

ACKNOWLEDGMENTS

From God, the Creator, to whose He created, I'm so grateful for the opportunity to live and work with creativity all around me.

Jes and Christine – the visionaries who dreamt up the concept and outline - and who encourage girls every day through dance, relationship, and inspiration.

Lauren, AJ, and Tony – for reading and re-reading multiple versions and providing loving suggestions.

North Jersey Christian Writers Group – who month after month, chapter by chapter provided valuable critique.

Beta readers – who kindly took time to read and share their comments for no reward other than this casual mention: Emily and Sam Irwin, Katie Sweeting, Jennifer Salzer-Alijewicz, Laura Madera

Editors extraordinaire – for wisdom, patience, helpfulness, and a wonderful, thorough job in a short amount of time: Sally Hanan of Inksnatchers and author Laura Hodges Poole

[1] Psalm 145:1
[2] Psalm 145:13,19

[3] Psalm 145:20
[4] Psalm 145:17-18
[5] Psalm 145:19
[6] 2 Kings 6:16
[7] Matthew 9:36
[8] Psalm 145:14
[9] John 6:68
[10] Mark 1:11
[11] 1 John 3:1
[12] Luke 1:38
[13] Romans 10:14-15

90505346R00078

Made in the USA
Columbia, SC
04 March 2018